THE CYCLE OF T
AND THE SEVEN LIBERAL ARTS

The Cycle of the Seasons and the Seven Liberal Arts

Sergei O. Prokofieff

TEMPLE LODGE
London

Translated by Richard Michell

Temple Lodge Publishing
51 Queen Caroline Street
London W6 9QL

Published by Temple Lodge 1995

Originally published in German under the title *Der Jahreskreislauf und die sieben Künste* by Verlag Freies Geistesleben, Stuttgart, 1994

A catalogue record for this book is available from the British Library

ISBN 0 904693 73 2

Cover by S. Gulbekian
Typeset by DP Photosetting, Aylesbury, Bucks
Printed and bound in Great Britain by Cromwell Press Limited, Broughton Gifford, Wiltshire

Contents

Preface

The following text reproduces the contents of a lecture that was held in several places. It was originally intended as a supplement to and continuation of my book *The Cycle of the Year as a Path of Initiation Leading to an Experience of the Christ Being—An Esoteric Study of the Festivals.*★ A knowledge of that book may therefore prove helpful in understanding the following presentation. But this can certainly be understood even without reading the book. An important basis for my talk was the lecture given by Rudolf Steiner on 29 December 1914 in Dornach on the impulses of transformation behind the artistic evolution of humanity (in *Art as Seen in the Light of Mystery Wisdom*, GA 275). The configuration of the various arts described therein and their connection with the constituent members of the human being provided me with the most important stimuli for my presentation.

Sergei O. Prokofieff
Stuttgart, 3 February 1994

★ Second English edition, Temple Lodge Publishing 1995.

The Cycle of the Seasons and the Seven Liberal Arts

One of the greatest mysteries of the passage of the seasons in the course of the year lies in its character as a living organism. It is evident that every living organism must express its life in a rhythmic way. We are familiar with many such rhythms in human life. One of the most important is that of breathing-in and breathing-out; another is the alternating rhythm of day and night. Spiritual science tells us that all four constituent members of the human being—the physical body, etheric body, astral body and ego—work together during the day. But their intimate connection is lost when the human being goes to sleep; the physical and etheric bodies then remain in bed while the astral body and ego ascend into the spiritual world. We can observe something similar, but on a far more comprehensive scale, in the life of the living organism that is our planet Earth. Terrestrial processes may also be regarded as a kind of breathing-in and breathing-out, or perhaps more strictly as a kind of going to sleep and waking up. And like man, the Earth also consists of four members in its waking state. Rudolf Steiner describes these processes in his lecture cycle *The Cycle of the Year as Breathing Process of the Earth.*[1] At the time of 'falling asleep' the soul and spirit of the Earth separate from their physical-etheric bodies and ascend, in like manner to the human being, into spiritual heights. But the Earth traverses in a yearly cycle what the human being goes through in a diurnal rhythm. The diurnal rhythm of the human being begins in the morning. Waking up is a process that can be compared to the beginning of life. This is followed by midday with its full expansion of life's forces, and an evening accompanied by tiredness and falling asleep that represents a little death in life. And in one of the seasons our Earth too undergoes a process that can be regarded as a waking up and thus in a certain sense as marking the beginning of the seasonal cycle. This is the autumn. In the autumn time the Earth begins to wake; it reaches its greatest wakefulness and highest level of consciousness during the Christmas period, and in the further course of the year it goes back to a sleep whose deepest point lies at the height of summer. So from a certain standpoint we can say that the life cycle of the Earth starts as it wakes in the autumn. This life cycle then follows its own laws, and the annual festivals of the Christian calendar stand as signposts along the path traversed by the seasons in the course of the year.

However, if we regard these great festivals not in isolation and separate from each other but as stations along an organic path unfolding throughout the year, then we must also start with the festival of autumn. And that means Michaelmas, the festival of Michael.

Michaelmas holds quite a special place within the entire cycle of the year's festivals. Whereas Anthroposophy brought renewal to the other festivals in the twentieth century, it gave the festival of Michael a true

basis for the first time, so that it may acquire its full
spiritual importance in the future. Rudolf Steiner often
pointed out that a new age of Michael began in the year
1879. Since then Michael has been the guiding spirit of
humanity, a task he will fulfil throughout the next three
to four centuries.[2] Rudolf Steiner also characterizes
Michael as that being whose principal function from the
earliest beginnings has been to govern the cosmic intelligence, in other words the cosmic thoughts of the
Hierarchies.[3] These thoughts formed the ground-plan of
the cosmos at the beginning of time and are revealed in
the all-encompassing architectonic pattern of the uni-
verse. Rudolf Steiner translated them into a form com-
prehensible to human beings and brought them to the
Earth as Anthroposophy. Seen in this way, Anthroposophy is cosmic intelligence apprehended by human
thoughts. If we acquire a feeling for the significance of
the intelligence governed by Michael, we can experience
our entire cosmos as a magnificent temple built up from
universal intelligence. We can then form the imagination
of how Michael performs a service of consecration at a
cosmic altar in the great solar temple of the world. He
stands before the countenances of the higher Hierarchies
as their servant and representative, and his service can be
seen as an essential part of the *cosmic ritual.* As a result of
this act of consecration, cosmic intelligence streams down
to the Earth as a consummate sacrifice, and Anthroposophy is a reflection of this process on the Earth. It
stands before us in its original form as a tremendous
cosmos of thoughts in which each part complements and
supports every other part, making it understandable and

capable of being apprehended by the ordinary consciousness of man. In this way, Anthroposophy can be
seen as a lofty work of art that can be compared to a kind
of architecture in thoughts. And yet this tremendous
structure of thoughts was not constructed in arbitrary
fashion but is a true image of the substantive architectonic
pattern of our cosmos. When experienced in such a living
way, Anthroposophy forms the first stage of the modern
path of initiation. In his *Occult Science*, Rudolf Steiner
spoke of 'the study of spiritual science, to which the pupil
initially applies himself with the powers of thought and
sound judgement acquired in the physical world'.[4]

Anthroposophy, understood as a reflection of the
entire spiritual cosmos in the sphere of thoughts, and at
the same time as a gift of Michael[5] to man through the
mediation of Rudolf Steiner, forms a sound basis for an
appropriate festival of Michael to arise in the future.
Rudolf Steiner often stressed that no clairvoyance is
required in order to found the festival of Michael.[6] This
contrasts with all the other annual festivals that originally
arose from the clairvoyant vision of ancient times. But it
cannot be brought about without an artistic sensibility
that evokes the feeling of how Anthroposophy is related
to the architectonic pattern of our cosmos and represents
its reflection in human thought. And if we call earthly
architecture a projection of the laws of the human physical body outwards, then Anthroposophy is the projection of cosmic laws into the interior of the human being,
or the projection of cosmic man into his inward self. It is
in this sense that Rudolf Steiner formulated the leitmotiv
for the future festival of Michael: 'Filled with ideas, the

soul experiences spirit-light when sense-appearance echoes in man as mere memory.'[7] Thus in the festival of Michael the soul that is filled with the thoughts of Anthroposophy experiences the light that radiates into human beings from the cosmic temple of Michael at this time.

★

According to *Occult Science*, the stage along the modern path of knowledge that follows the period of study is 'the attainment of imaginative cognition'.[8] But there is a very important intermediate position between these two stages. And in order to understand it better we must take a closer look at the way that thinking works in the human being. Our thinking has its original source in the astral body. But it enters our consciousness only if it is reflected by the physical body. The thinking that takes place in the astral body and is reflected by the physical body makes use of the power of sound judgement 'that has been acquired in the physical world'. Equipped with this thinking, we can continue to pursue our study of Anthroposophy until we experience it as a magnificent thought structure that corresponds to a higher reality. But we can proceed to take a further step along this path. We can make our thinking come alive by transferring the process of reflection from the physical body to the etheric body. The processes that take place in our astral body are then reflected into our consciousness by the etheric body and not the physical body. Such an inward constitution of thinking was possessed in great perfection by Goethe. A significant reason for this lay in one of his earlier incarnations, when he lived as a sculptor in ancient Greece during the time of Plato.[9] By activating this thinking, he was able to speak from his own experience about the archetypal plant and the principle of metamorphosis. Although he did not yet possess a fully developed imaginative clairvoyance—he saw neither the group-souls of the plants nor elemental beings—this was not our ordinary thinking either. Living thinking differs from the latter in that it not only apprehends *existing* thoughts but begins to fashion thoughts plastically out of an inner activity. However, this process does not take place according to the physical laws of reasonable logic and causality, but follows the etheric laws of metamorphosis. By bringing this very much stronger inward activity to bear, the soul deals with thoughts in the same way as a sculptor handles clay.

So this strengthened thinking represents a kind of inward sculpting. Let us recall that architecture is the projection of the laws of the physical body outwards and sculpture the projection of the laws of the etheric body outwards. We may then regard classical Greek sculpture as producing the most beautiful creations in this sense. They represent the visible manifestation of the pure etheric forces of the human being. That is why they are so chaste and innocent of passion. For a classical sculptor was trained in the Greek Mysteries to master his astral body so that nothing flowed from it into the pure image of the etheric forces that he expressed in stone or clay. Whenever we find a passionate (astral) element in Hellenic sculpture, we are looking at works that have already transgressed the boundary of the true ideas of beauty held

The priest Laocoön and his sons are crushed by the serpents of
Poseidon. Around 30 BC Vatican Museum, Rome

by the Greeks.[10] We see such works in the *Laocoön* (see photograph on p. 15) or in the various representations of the demonic, for example. The altar at Pergamon is a fine example of the latter (see photograph below). Here, the struggle between the gods and the Titans shows the former as being completely dispassionate, whereas the latter are depicted as being agitated by the instinctive forces of a demonic astrality.

This elimination of the lower astral from the etheric is also necessary for living thinking. For if the thinker is to approach the real mysteries of nature with living thinking he must not form his thoughts in an arbitrary manner, but must prepare something like an arena within his mind upon which the facts of the world can express themselves

Athena group. East side of the Pergamon altar.
Pergamon Museum, Berlin

untrammelled. In this sense, a purified and tamed astral body is one of the most important preconditions not only for living thinking as such but quite generally for entering rightly into the imaginative world. Thus Rudolf Steiner once said that Goethe was tainted only to a very small extent with the luciferic element.[11] In ancient Greece, the word catharsis was used to designate the attainment of selflessness in the astral body. To help us achieve this state, the wonderful wisdom of world guidance has introduced the four weeks of Advent, or the weeks of 'awaiting' into the cycle of the year. In these weeks before Christmas, the human being can practise attaining selflessness in his astral body: the selflessness of willing in the first week, of willing and feeling in the second week, and of willing, feeling and thinking in the third week. In other words: control of the actions in the first week, control of the feelings in the second week and control of the thoughts in the third week. For it is these three elements that make up the life of the human astral body.

If the human being has reached a certain stage of selflessness in his astral body during the first three weeks of Advent he is inwardly ready to enter the world of objective Imagination in the fourth week. For he has then gained the power not only to have his thinking reflected by his etheric body but of apprehending it directly in his astral body. He then experiences consciously what he otherwise goes through unconsciously during the sleep state when he dwells outside his physical and etheric bodies. This amounts to nothing less than entering the world of the objective Imagination, the world from which the human soul descends to Earth through birth.

From thence also came the paradisaic being who became the bearer of the Christ. So it follows that it is easier to enter the imaginative world at Christmas than at any other time of the year. And the entry will take place in a particularly harmonious way if the first thing the pupil experiences in the imaginative world is the imagination of Christmas: the Virgin with the Child on her lap. In this imagination, her countenance can be seen to reflect the entire starry cosmos that we have come to perceive as the great temple of the world. And the Child that she bears on her lap is the manifestation of the etheric forces of the Sun, the forces of the original etheric body of humanity known in the Bible as the Tree of Life.[12] Further down, the rich folds of her garment express the subdued and purified Moon forces, the forces of a human astral body that has undergone the complete process of catharsis.

This imagination can arise in a real way within the human soul at Christmas if the astral body was sufficiently purified during Advent. Its appearance can be taken as a sign of enlightenment or *photismos* in the sense of the ancient Mysteries. In a certain manner, this imagination is a revelation of a purified astral body that is ready to receive a higher life and offer it an appropriate matrix. This is why the completely purified astral body was called the Virgin Sophia from the earliest times among the groups associated with esoteric Christianity.[13] The art of painting constitutes a reflection in the terrestrial world of spiritual imaginations, and it can attain its greatest heights when it is able to depict spiritual processes in the purified astral body. This is how Raphael's *Sistine Madonna* originated, for example.[14]

★

However, the pupil may go through all three of these stages without feeling any really dramatic effects upon his inner life. A human being may even be granted these imaginations in such a way that they have a harmonizing and supportive effect on his life. Thus one may meet people today who can perceive elemental spirits or etheric processes in nature, and thereby gain comfort and assurance in their lives. But this calm character changes immediately as soon as clairvoyance is transformed into true initiation.[15] For initiation brings the human being in touch not only with the past but also with the future. And the latter always bears a dramatic character. To know the future, the pupil must cross the threshold to the spiritual world in full consciousness, and must build a bridge over the abyss of existence by his own power. This abyss, which separates an incipient clairvoyance from the first stages of initiation, lies between the stages of Imagination and Inspiration. For this reason Rudolf Steiner said that *genuine* initiation begins with the stage of Inspiration.[16] Another name for it is 'the reading of the hidden script'.[17] The difficulty that the pupil encounters at this point is already apparent from the way that Rudolf Steiner characterizes the transition from Imagination to Inspiration. For at this juncture the pupil must extirpate from his consciousness everything that he had created at the imaginative stage, and must have the strength of will to withstand a completely empty consciousness without losing himself in non-existence.[18]

One of the best-known works by Friedrich Nietzsche is *The Birth of Tragedy from the Spirit of Music*. Here we may say the inverse, that the birth of music takes place from the spirit of tragedy. The experience of the abyss is associated with the transition from spiritual space to the stream of spiritual time, and that means entry into the true spiritual world which the soul may otherwise experience in this form only after death. This can be done today thanks to the deed of the Christ, who brought the impulse of spiritualized time into the dying spatial conditions of the Earth through his incarnation in a human body.[19] This has made it possible for the spiritual seeker to ascend consciously beyond the sphere of Imagination into that of Inspiration. In this loftier sphere the pupil experiences the revelation of his higher ego, which sounds forth in the world of powerful cosmic inspirations, for the first time. This higher ego then appears, itself resounding, as if from the world-encompassing ocean of the harmonies of the spheres, whose last echo could still be heard by the Pythagoreans. This experience can be reproduced on Earth only by the art of music. Through music, the human ego reveals itself in the astral body. An image of this process is presented by Orpheus, who tames the savage beasts—the instinctive forces of the astral body—by playing his lyre, bringing them peace, harmony and transformation from out of his ego.

Within the cycle of the year, the experience of the abyss of existence and the associated transformation of consciousness are characterized by the Twelve Holy Nights that mark the path from Jesus to Christ, from the human to the divine in ourselves, to the first encounter with the higher Ego.

The abyss that lies between Christmas and Epiphany

and represents the gulf between man and God can be overcome only when Christ, the only God who became man, comes to the aid of man. This help is forthcoming by penetrating into the mystery of His incarnation, which occurred at the baptism in the Jordan and forms the inner content of the festival of the Epiphany.

In the last lecture of the cycle *True and False Paths in Spiritual Investigation*,[20] Rudolf Steiner speaks of how in the future music will be the only art capable of representing the mystery of the incarnation of God at the Jordan: the secret of the union of the divine Ego, at first with the astral body of a human being and then with his two other sheaths. For it is only because God became man at this point in human development that man may now find the right path into the divine world.

Two things make it evident that the baptism at the Jordan involves not only imaginations but above all inspirations. The first is the voice from Heaven saying, 'This is my Son filled with my love, in whom I reveal myself,'[21] and the second is that the imaginations associated with the baptism assume forms derived from the animal world. Pure imaginations can be expressed only by plant forms. If, however, they are permeated by inspirations, they assume forms such as those of the dove or lamb that were revealed to John's clairvoyant vision (John 1:29, 32).[22]

★

But the higher Ego described here in its first manifestation does not yet reveal itself fully. This occurs only at the next stage along the path of initiation, namely, that of

Intuition. In his book *The Threshold of the Spiritual World*[23] Rudolf Steiner writes about the three principal aspects of the human ego: the everyday ego, the 'other' or 'higher' ego and the 'true' ego of man. They are reflected in the three primal images of Christmas, Epiphany and Easter, which represent the three stages of the union of the Christ with human existence.

In *Occult Science*, Rudolf Steiner describes how only in Intuition can the Mystery of Golgotha become a personal experience for the pupil of the spirit.[24] Only in Intuition can the Mystery of the Logos, the Word, be understood. For in this Logos the forces of all nine Hierarchies manifest in the spiritual world, as Rudolf Steiner indicated in the fourth verse of the Foundation Stone Meditation that he gave at the Christmas Conference on Saturday 29 December 1923.[25] We may also say that the First and highest Hierarchy reveals itself in the Cosmic Word essentially in a *dramatic* manner as in thunder and lightning, the Second in an *epic* way, and the Third, which penetrates into the interior of man, acts in a *lyric* manner. The Mystery of Golgotha now links this concert of the Hierarchies with the Earth, thus forming the basis for the future art of recitation, where the word works magically in the world as a creative giver of life. Thus Rudolf Steiner once said that in the future the human being would become a micrologos, a true image of the Macrologos.[26] For this reason, it is precisely recitation— the art of the word—that can approach most closely to the mysteries of Golgotha. The works of this art form stand like great milestones in the history of humanity, and through them human beings can acquire an understanding of the full significance of the Mystery of Golgotha. Chief among them are the Gospel of St John and, in our time, the Foundation Stone Meditation by Rudolf Steiner. All this is linked in the profoundest way with the unfolding of the basic impulse of the Mysteries of the Grail. Rudolf Steiner describes how these Mysteries will allow the human being to transform his larynx in the distant future to create a new organ of reproduction through which he can bring forth his kind in a spiritual way.[27] The human being will then be able to work creatively into physical matter itself through the word alone. Rudolf Steiner describes this ideal with the words: 'And the time must come when the flesh will again become word and will learn to dwell in the kingdom of the word.'[28] A preliminary stage towards this distant future will be the appearance of the Maitreya Buddha 3000 years hence. Rudolf Steiner tells us that 'his words will immediately become moral impulses in human beings who hear them by virtue of their magical power'.[29]

The first steps towards this great future were made by founding the new art of speech formation from out of Anthroposophy. In this art, the word of man develops powers that can have an etheric-moral effect.

After Intuition, the pupil of the spirit moves to still higher stages along the path of initiation. The reader will find a description of these in connection with the annual festivals in the author's book *The Cycle of the Year as a Path of Initiation Leading to an Experience of the Christ Being.*[30] But let us now consider the relation between the annual festivals and the various arts. From what has already been said we can see that the arts represent true paths to a knowledge of the great world mysteries that are revealed in the main festivals of the year. Goethe already indicated this property of art when he spoke of beauty as being a 'manifestation of secret laws of nature . . . that would have remained hidden from us for ever without its appearance'.[31]

★

In the cycle of the year, Easter is followed by the festival of the Ascension. To gain a better understanding of this event, we must look at the human etheric body. This harbours two tendencies: firstly the inborn striving to unite with the great Sun-sphere from which it originated; and secondly a more material tendency by virtue of which the materialistic thoughts and feelings of today's human beings bind it to the Earth and separate it from its cosmic homeland. The human etheric body then becomes increasingly similar to the physical body and takes up the forces of death from it. If either tendency were to dominate, the human being would be unable to complete his further evolution on the Earth. If the etheric body were to follow its tendency towards the Sun, it would become impossible for man to acquire an individual existence on the Earth. And if the etheric body were to take up these powerful forces of death, humanity would be condemned to die out on Earth. To allow human beings to continue dwelling on the Earth, a way had to be found of obtaining the full measure of the cosmic forces originally belonging to the etheric body from the Sun-sphere as a counterweight to the forces of death. But this had to happen on the Earth itself, not in separation from it. This possibility was created by the Ascension of Christ.

The imagination that underlies this festival shows how the Christ Being unites Himself with the tendency of the human etheric body towards the Sun. Although remaining in the sphere of the Earth, he then imparts to the etheric body those sidereal and planetary forces that it previously possessed directly only in the Sun-sphere.[32] This process forms the basis for another art form, one that has only been created now, in the twentieth century. This is the art of eurythmy. It cannot be truly understood without entering into the Mystery of the Ascension in the way already described. This is because eurythmy already reveals to us on the Earth those cosmic laws working in the human etheric body that entered into it through the Ascension of the Christ and whose deeper nature is linked to the development of the Life Spirit. In this respect, eurythmy is naturally only at the beginning of its development. Rudolf Steiner points to this when he says that today it 'can naturally be only a babbling compared to what must one day arise from this art form'.[33] It is nonetheless extremely important to bear these relationships in our awareness, for they can provide a sound basis for acquiring the necessary responsibility towards this art form that owes its origin directly to the Christ Mystery.

★

The next festival after Ascension is Whitsun (Pentecost). Another great art form is associated with it: the art of social harmony, the social skilfulness that gives rise to a true community of free spirits.[34] This is shown in a wonderful way in the imagination of the Whitsun event. It lets us recall the beginnings of the original community in which all twelve main currents of humanity come together in a complete and harmonious confluence of their individualized representatives. This primal image of a community of the future at the same time gives us a prophetic picture of the highest achievement of the art of social harmony. Thus the Whitsun imagination shows us how the spirit descends upon each human being individually in tongues of flame. This is why Rudolf Steiner once called this spirit an individualized spirit.[35] For each of the twelve apostles receives his own spiritual impulse, and yet it is always the same spirit. The greatest opposition in the more recent life of humanity, that between individualization and community, is thus bridged prophetically at the highest spiritual level. The first shoots of the future development of Spirit Man then appear in such a community. Its members are those human beings who have received the baptism of fire and the spirit proclaimed by Christ (John 1:27). It is the realization of the great ideal of the brotherhood of human beings imbued by a single spirit over the whole Earth. Rudolf Steiner points to this ideal in his *Philosophy of Freedom* when he says that two truly free human beings will never find themselves in disharmony or contradiction.

Seen from a more esoteric angle, this global Whitsun community will lead to a completely new ordering of karma within humanity. The power of the Christ, as the Lord of Karma, will then restore the harmony between karma and the laws of the spiritual cosmos. This will in no way constrain the will of man, but will lead to a complete development of human freedom into the cosmic dimension. Rudolf Steiner indicates this development with the following words: 'It is not the way of the spiritual world to unite the karma of the individual with overall karma in an arbitrary way, but so that the organic structure of the community comes to reflect the order in the heavens ... this is essentially the foundation of a future humanity based on the ego nature.'[36]

The description given above shows us how deeply the arts of man are connected with the world mysteries and with the annual festivals. When these seven arts are experienced in the cycle of the year in the way presented, they come to resemble the seven stars carried in the hand of the Son of Man as described in the Apocalypse.

★

Now only one more great festival remains: the summer festival of St John—also known as Midsummer's Day or the festival of St John the Baptist. At this time, the Earth has fully breathed out its soul and spirit. It is in a state of deepest sleep that manifests in the wonderfully developed nature of high summer. All that was essentially formed and guided by the forces of the seven planets during the rest of the year is now united with the powers coming from the realm of the fixed stars through the mediation of the Sun. For the physical and etheric bodies of the Earth can continue to exist while their soul and spirit dwell in the spiritual world only because they are borne by the highest Hierarchy from beyond the planetary world. The same thing occurs as with the sleeping human being, but now at a macrocosmic level. For the highest spiritual beings also send their forces into man while his spiritual-soul nature sojourns outside his physical-etheric bodies at night. And we see that all the seven arts described so far—as well as the cosmic forces underlying them—must be brought to a higher harmony at this concluding stage, exactly as the courses of the seven planets are surrounded by the sphere of the zodiac.

But what art form could be still higher, still more comprehensive than the seven already mentioned? What art can comprehend all the seven stages described so far in the manner of an octave?

We have seen how all seven arts are linked to certain cosmic activities that come to fitting expression in the annual festivals. And yet we have not spoken only of the seven earthly arts but also about their spiritual sources, their cosmic origins. We firstly indicated the architectonic pattern of the cosmic thoughts, then the plastic formative forces of the cosmos—the sphere of the cosmic imagination or cosmic painting—and then the Music of the Cosmos or the Spheres—the Cosmic Word—followed by the cosmic sources of eurythmy that arose from the confluence of all the forces of the etheric cosmos. Finally we spoke of the art of social harmony whose origin is to be sought in the co-operation between human beings who are aware of their cosmic origin. But what unites all these seven activities? It is their cosmic origin and character, and from this there follows an eighth, concluding art form that is at the same time the highest of them all: the art of living in harmony with the entire cosmos. We may then say that all the other cosmic-terrestrial arts rest within this last art form as in a mighty lap. And the most obvious way of practising this highest of the arts is consciously to experience the cycle of the year and to participate in the annual festivals. Their aim is to give us an ever more intensive experience of the Christ Being as the new Spirit of the Earth who brought the cosmic forces to our planet in their fullness.

But there is another aspect of the festival of St John that perhaps brings out most clearly its special position within the cycle of the year. For this festival commemorates the birth of the oldest human individuality, who appears at the Turning-point of Time by the name of John the Baptist.[37] He is the last great prophet of the old world and at the same time the first proclaimer of the new Christian age. His entire world-encompassing wisdom, still coming from the sphere of the Father, gave rise to his famous words 'He must increase, but I must decrease' (John 3:30). That means that the small, limited, terrestrial human being must decline, but the coming, cosmic man of the future must grow. We hear the great affirmation by man at the end of the pre-Christian epoch, even before the Mystery of Golgotha. We find these words again in the Christian period, but in totally refashioned form. What John the Baptist proclaimed as the purest revelation of the Father forces sounds forth to us, now reborn from the forces of the Son, in the new words of the Apostle Paul: 'Not I, but Christ in me' (Galatians 2:20). Not the small, limited, earthly human being, but cosmic man, the Christ in me. The words of John are reborn from the sphere of the Son, of the Christ.

But these words have now gone through a third metamorphosis, precisely in our own time. They were reborn once more in the twentieth century, but now not from the Father forces alone nor from those of the Son alone but from the forces of the Spirit that unite the forces of Father and Son. Rudolf Steiner gave utterance to these words as the first guideline, a formula that he used to describe the essential nature of Anthroposophy from out of the spirit: 'Anthroposophy is a path of knowledge that aims to lead the spiritual in man to the spiritual in the cosmos. It arises in the human being as a need of the heart and the feelings.'[38] The conscious experience of the annual cycle of the year and its festivals is the surest way of leading the spiritual in the human being to the spiritual in the cosmos. It unites Anthroposophy with the entire development of Christianity on our Earth. In this sense, Rudolf Steiner tells us that the aim of Anthroposophy is to partake of the destiny of Christianity.[39]

The arts have been characterized by a strong element of community-building at all times. We can deepen and strengthen this impulse significantly today by establishing a connection between the various arts and the cycle of the year and its festivals. In this way the arts will increasingly be able to unite human beings with their cosmic origin and contribute to the central tasks of Anthroposophy already described. They will thus come into a harmonious relation with science, as they draw their inspirations from the natural cycle of the seasons, but will also establish a connection to the religious impulses sorely needed by modern man by means of the annual festivals. (The term 'religious' does not refer to any particular religion, but indicates that these impulses arise directly from a conscious association with cosmic existence within the cycle of the seasons. The origin of the Latin word *religio* also points to such a renewed connection between the human being and a divine element. It was already linked with *religare*, to bind together or tie up, in the early Christian period). The great ideal of the synthesis of science, art and religion, already prepared over the centuries in the true Rosicrucian communities, can then increasingly become a reality.

As they work towards this ideal, human beings will prepare themselves consciously to cross the threshold to the spiritual world, not only as individual pupils of the spirit but as an entire community. In the course of time, a community or association will arise on the Earth that dwells in full harmony with the cosmic-spiritual forces and is able to draw its power directly from the cosmos, thus forming a cosmic gateway upon the Earth. Rudolf Steiner used the term 'inverse ritual' to designate such an association with cosmic existence.[40] No longer do Angels descend to men, but men ascend to Angels from whom they obtain the impulses they will increasingly need to build an existence that is worthy of human beings and to heal the Earth. Such a community will form a gateway through which cosmic forces can flow directly into the life of the Earth, transforming and renewing all things. And the human being will be imbued increasingly with the feeling that he is indeed embedded in the stream of cosmic events as an individual, but in community with those harbouring similar strivings.

This feeling can also give those human beings connected with Anthroposophy the courage and strength to accomplish in the world all that must be fulfilled today from the true Michaelic *spirit of the times.*

Supplementary Reflections

As we look at the cycle of the year, we can experience it as a living process of respiration that resembles the human process of breathing-in and breathing-out.

The breathing-in of the Earth organism corresponds to the declining half of the year from high summer through autumn to winter, whereas its breathing-out takes place in the other half of the year from winter through spring to summer. Breathing-in is associated with the entire past of humanity, for the declining year represents the entry into matter of the soul and spirit all the way to the processes of nature. It is the path of the spirit becoming flesh. This process contains the great wisdom laid into it by the Hierarchies in the past, but it is insufficient to overcome the increasingly powerful forces of death prevailing in human beings and in nature. Neither can the thoughts and concepts grasped during this time be wrested from the forces of death unless they are enlivened by a developed thinking imbued with an architectonic-plastic-pictorial or imaginative character. Thus the autumn reveals to us the great beauty of a past, dying world. But this dying away is also associated with the individualization of the human being. As an individual, man tries to save this beautiful and wise old world-order from dying away. He does this through the arts that belong to this half of the year and its festivals: the arts of space. Architecture reveals the laws of the physical body, sculpture those of the etheric body, and painting those of the astral body. By overcoming death, however, the Christ has given this past a future. Thus the arts of time in the other half of the year gain a new significance that points into the future. Music, recitation, eurythmy and the art of social harmony no longer merely bring the past to life, they are on the way to becoming co-creators of nature. Just as the three spatial arts constitute a remembrance of how humanity issues forth from the cosmic spheres, the temporal arts are an anticipation of how humankind returns to the cosmos after having undergone an evolution. This process corresponds to the ascending half of the year. It describes the natural separation of the spiritual-soul element from physical matter and its ascent into cosmic existence. This is the path into the future; the forces of death working in nature and in man are overcome by the spirit, the dying flesh becomes transfigured into spirit. This process is no longer associated with wisdom, but with the will and the life within it. Thus the arts of music, recitation, eurythmy and social harmony shall fashion the seeds of the future lying dormant in this will and wake them to new life. The process of individualization characterizing the other half of the year contrasts sharply with this social impulse that gives us a first glimpse of the beauty of a future world. Through it, the human being lays the foundations for a new cosmos. Rudolf Steiner once said that the declining half of the year is connected with the forces of karma.[41] In karma the past is preserved. The spatial arts also have this character; once created, they remain in existence in the world. The other half of the year is associated with freedom. It manifests in the temporal arts, whose expression is always associated with man's direct activity and cannot exist without that activity.

Music takes up a middle position within the seven arts. In dance it tends towards the spatial arts and in singing towards the temporal ones, thus forming a bridge between the two.

Thus the spatial arts bring to expression a last echo from a time when the human being was still guided by the Hierarchies in the absence of his own activity. And the temporal arts give us some idea of what will emerge in the future from the free initiative of human beings, also in the social sphere.

★

But we should not omit a still deeper aspect underlying the cycle of the seasons and its main festivals. For the great festivals of the year are also an earthly reflection of ritual events that have their origin in the world of the Hierarchies. In the ascending scale of the divine-spiritual Hierarchies we can firstly distinguish the Angels, who guide individual human beings, then the Archangels, who are the guides of the various peoples of the Earth, followed by the Archai, who guide all of humanity from epoch to epoch. Among the Archai we also find Michael, the leading Time Spirit of our present epoch with whose festival we began our consideration of the festivals of the year. Of these three types of spiritual being, it is especially the Archai who perform a service of sacrifice to the

Hierarchies yet higher up the scale. Thus behind the festival of Michael we have the sacrificial deeds offered by the beings belonging to the Hierarchy of the Archai to the next highest Hierarchy, the Spirits of Form. This activity gives rise to a cosmic image of the art of architecture. Another sacrifice of this kind lies behind the period of Advent: the one offered by the Spirits of Form to the Spirits of Movement. This process is reflected in the art of sculpture as a transition from the world of form to the world of movement. In the same way, Christmas is underlain by the sacrificial deeds wrought by the Spirits of Movement and offered up to the Spirits of Wisdom. These are brought to purest expression in the imagination of the Divine Sophia, the cosmic wisdom.

The Spirits of Wisdom work together with the Thrones in the activity underlying the festival of the Epiphany. In describing the baptism in the Jordan, the Gospels speak of the voice from the exalted sphere of the Father. This is the sphere from which the first incarnation of our Earth issued forth by virtue of the sacrifice of the Spirits of Will. The opening verses of the Gospel of St John point to this primal beginning. In our planetary system, the Spirits of Will or Thrones are associated with the Saturn-sphere. The next Hierarchy, the Cherubim, extends beyond it and works from the pure world of the stars. This power of the fixed stars is revealed in the resurrection body of the Christ, which we may therefore call a sidereal body. Thus behind the events of Easter we see a confluence of the pure sacrificial activity of the Thrones and the Cherubim. In contrast, the activity underlying the imagination of the Ascension is not associated with any of the planetary spheres. There, the pure sidereal beings of the Cherubim sacrifice themselves to the still higher sidereal beings of the Seraphim. Thus we must seek the primal image of the Ascension in the pure starry sphere that also includes the highest aspect of the Sun in its character as a fixed star.

At Whitsun, the Seraphim turn to the realm lying above the hierarchical cosmos and known in Christian esotericism as the sphere of the Holy Spirit. From it they receive the spiritual impulses that can work through all the Hierarchies below them as far as earthly conditions. Finally, at St John's the entire Earth opens up to the forces coming from the super-hierarchical sphere. For this reason, Rudolf Steiner associates St John's with the revelation of the Trinity.[42] The Spirit goes forth from the Son, who fills Himself entirely with the forces of the Father. This highest sphere is reflected *in earthly existence* by the third Hierarchy, so that the Angels bring humanity the impulses of the Spirit, the Archangels those of the Son and the Archai those of the Father. In this way the transition takes place from St John's to Michaelmas, where the substance received from above in the depths begins its way upwards through the further cycle of the year in the sense of the enduring ritual. At Michaelmas, the Archai sacrifice themselves to the Spirits of Form, at Advent the Spirits of Form to the Spirits of Movement and so forth.

Thus the cycle of the year and its seven festivals give us a primal image and a revelation of what may be called the great cosmic ritual that is performed unceasingly in the world of the Hierarchies.

Notes

Quotations giving no references to an author are taken from the works of Rudolf Steiner.

GA = *Gesamtausgabe*. Reference is to the volume number from the catalogue of the collected edition of Rudolf Steiner's works in the original German (published by Rudolf Steiner Verlag, Switzerland).

RSP = Rudolf Steiner Press, London
AP = Anthroposophic Press, New York
APC = Anthroposophical Publishing Co, London
GAR = Garber Communications Inc., Blauvelt, NY

1 *The Cycle of the Year as Breathing Process of the Earth*, lecture cycle from 31 March–8 April 1923, AP 1984, and *Michaelmas and the Soul-Forces of Man*, lecture cycle from 27 September to 1 October 1923, AP 1982 (GA 223).

2 *Karmic Relationships*, Vol. 6, lecture of 19 July 1924 (GA 240), RSP 1989. And: *True and False Paths in Spiritual Investigation*, lecture of 18 August 1924 (GA 243), RSP 1985.

3 Lecture of 19 July 1924. See Note 2.

4 *Occult Science—An Outline*, Chapter V, 'Knowledge of Higher Worlds' (GA 13), RSP 1984.

5   Rudolf Steiner spoke about spiritual knowledge as 'the gift of Michael' on 2 May 1913, in *Occult Science and Occult Development. Christ at the Time of the Mystery of Golgotha* (GA 152), RSP 1983.

6   Lecture of 28 September 1923 (GA 223), in *Anthroposophy and the Human Gemüt*, AP 1946, reprinted under the title *Michaelmas and the Soul Forces of Man*, AP 1982.

7   *Anthroposophical Leading Thoughts*, 'Man in his Macrocosmic Being' (GA 26), RSP 1985.

8   See Note 4.

9   *The Mysteries of the East and of Christianity*, lecture of 7 February 1913 (GA 144), GAR 1989.

10 *The Nature and Origin of the Arts*, lecture of 28 October 1909 (GA 271), APC, no date.

11 *Social Understanding through Spiritual Scientific Knowledge*, lecture of 15 November 1909 (GA 191), AP 1982.

12 *The Gospel of St Luke*, lecture of 21 September 1909 (GA 114), RSP 1988.

13 *The Gospel of St John*, lecture of 31 May 1908 (GA 103), AP 1984.

14 On the origin of Raphael's *Sistine Madonna*, see S.O. Prokofieff, *Eternal Individuality. Towards a Karmic Biography of Novalis*, Temple Lodge Publishing 1993.

15 On the difference between clairvoyance and initiation, see Chapter 2 of *The Spiritual Guidance of Humanity* (GA 15), AP 1992.

16 That the boundary between clairvoyance and initiation in the true sense runs between imaginative and inspired cognition can also be seen from Rudolf Steiner's lecture of 15 September 1909, in *The Gospel of St Luke* (GA 114), RSP 1988.

17 See Note 4.

18   See Note 4.

19   More details on this point can be found in *Karmic Relationships*, Vol. 2, in the lecture of 4 June 1924 (GA 236), RSP 1984.

20   *True and False Paths in Spiritual Investigation*, lecture of 22 August 1924 (GA 243), RSP 1985.

21   Matthew 3:17. This is the way that Rudolf Steiner translates the text in his lecture of 3 July 1909, in *The Gospel of St John and its Relation to the Other Three Gospels* (GA 112), AP 1982.

22   *The Mystery of the Trinity*, lecture of 28 July 1922 (GA 214), AP 1991.

23   *A Road to Self Knowledge and The Threshold of the Spiritual World*, chapter entitled 'Man's True Ego' (GA 17), RSP 1990.

24   See Note 4.

25   *The Christmas Conference for the Founding of the General Anthroposophical Society, 1923/24* (GA 260), AP 1990. See also S.O. Prokofieff, *Rudolf Steiner and the Founding of the New Mysteries*, Chapter 5, Temple Lodge Publishing 1994.

26   *Mystery Knowledge and Mystery Centres*, lecture of 2 December 1923 (GA 232), GAR 1989.

27   *Occult Signs and Symbols*, lecture of 29 December 1907 (GA 101), AP 1990.

28   *The Mission of the Archangel Michael*, lecture of 22 November 1919 (GA 194), AP 1961.

29   *Esoteric Christianity and the Mission of Christian Rosenkreutz*, lecture of 21 September 1911 (GA 130), RSP 1984.

30   S.O. Prokofieff, *The Cycle of the Year as a Path of Initiation Leading to an Experience of the Christ Being*, Temple Lodge Publishing 1995.

31. J.W. Goethe, *Maximen und Reflexionen* (Maxims and Reflections), Hamburg edition, Vol. 12, p.467.
32 *The Festivals and their Meaning*, lecture of 7 May 1923 (GA 224), RSP 1981. Rudolf Steiner also speaks of the processes of hardening and desiccation in the human etheric body during the fifth post-Atlantean epoch in *The Balance in the World and Man*, lecture of 20 November 1914 (GA 158), AP 1977.
33 *Art as Seen in the Light of Mystery Wisdom*, lecture of 29 December 1914 (GA 275), RSP 1984.
34 The foundation for this highest of the arts was already created by Rudolf Steiner in the second part of his *Philosophy of Freedom* (1894) (GA 4), RSP 1988.
35 *The Reappearance of Christ in the Etheric*, lecture of 15 May 1910, AP 1983.
36 *The Gospel of St Matthew*, lecture of 11 September 1910 (GA 123), RSP 1985.
37 *The Gospel of St John*, lecture of 22 May 1908 (GA 103), AP 1984.
38 First 'leading thought' in *Anthroposophical Leading Thoughts* (GA 26), RSP 1985.
39 *Man's Being, his Destiny and World Evolution*, address in Christiania (Oslo), 17 May 1923 (GA 226), AP 1984.
40 *Awakening to Community*, lecture of 3 March 1923 (GA 257), AP 1974.
41 *Karmic Relationships*, Vol. 2, lecture of 4 June 1924 (GA 236), RSP 1974.
42 *The Four Seasons and the Archangels*, lecture of 12 October 1923 (GA 229), RSP 1984.

THE CYCLE OF THE YEAR AS A PATH OF INITIATION LEADING TO AN EXPERIENCE OF THE CHRIST BEING

Sergei O. Prokofieff

In ancient times humanity possessed an innate knowledge of the spiritual foundations of existence. Such knowledge could be acquired through inwardly accompanying the cycle of the year and the great seasonal festivals connected to it. But this instinctive knowledge had to be lost in order that human beings could discover individual freedom. In our time, as Prokofieff demonstrates in this comprehensive work, 'this knowledge must be found anew through the free, light-filled consciousness of the fully developed human personality'.

By following the spiritual path of the cycle of the year, Prokofieff penetrates to the deeper esoteric realities of the seven Christian festivals of Michaelmas, Christmas, Epiphany, Easter, Ascension, Whitsun, and St John's Tide. Basing his research on the work of the twentieth-century initiate Rudolf Steiner, he shows that these festivals are spiritual facts which exist independently of religious traditions and cultural customs.

Working with the festivals in an esoteric sense can provide a true path of initiation, enabling the individual ultimately to experience the being of the earth, Christ. Thus, the journey of study through this book can lead the reader to an experience of the modern Christian-Rosicrucian path, along which 'it is possible to take the first steps towards life in partnership with the course of cosmic existence'.

496 pp; 24 × 16 cm; hardback; ISBN 0 904693 70 8

THE TWELVE HOLY NIGHTS AND THE SPIRITUAL HIERARCHIES

Sergei O. Prokofieff

A rich source of inspiration for those wishing to penetrate the mysteries of the Twelve Holy Nights, and an impressive blend of scholarship and original spiritual research. Prokofieff draws on the whole extent of Rudolf Steiner's work to form an intricate picture of the cosmic forces at play between Christmas and Epiphany.

We are guided imaginatively through the interior of the First Goetheanum—Steiner's architectural masterpiece destroyed by fire in 1922—whose structure and decorations are seen to constitute a coherent esoteric map. Our task now, suggests Prokofieff, is to build the First Goetheanum once again in ourselves and, through a new schooling of the etheric, strive for a truly twentieth century Way of Initiation.

This second edition includes revisions and additions.

208 pp; 22 × 14 cm; hardback; ISBN 0 904693 54 6

THE OCCULT SIGNIFICANCE OF FORGIVENESS

Sergei O. Prokofieff

The twentieth century, filled with turmoil and war, is littered with angry and bitter feelings. Modern legalistic thinking—largely preoccupied with finding and proving guilt—only exacerbates this situation. Yet many individuals, sincerely wishing to break the never-ending cycle of recrimination, are asking: 'What can I do to change and improve the world?'

Prokofieff shows how, in our personal and moral lives, the forces which lead to 'forgiveness' may be consciously and freely developed. Without preaching a morality of forgiveness, he sets before us the spiritual facts which speak for themselves. The importance of the theme becomes apparent—not simply for personal salvation, but for the furtherance of humanity's evolution . . .

From Tsarist Russia to the concentration camps of Nazi Germany, the author gives striking examples of people who have been able to forgive terrible crimes. His rich analysis delves beneath the immediately perceptible, revealing the esoteric significance of every single act of true forgiveness.

'. . . *Sergei Prokofieff reaches from the intimacies of daily life to the most sacred realities.*
This is an important work, which deserves to be fully grasped and taken to heart.'
—Anthroposophy Today

208 pp; 22 × 14 cm; hardback; ISBN 0 904693 71 6

RUDOLF STEINER AND THE FOUNDING OF THE NEW MYSTERIES

Sergei O. Prokofieff

In the new Introduction, hitherto unpublished in English, Prokofieff describes the events in his life which led to his discovery of the work of Rudolf Steiner—then proscribed by the Bolshevik dictatorship—and how he came to write *Rudolf Steiner and the Founding of the New Mysteries* while living in Soviet Russia. The resulting book—an esoteric study of Rudolf Steiner and Anthroposophy, unprecedented in its depth and significance—was first published in Germany in 1982 and met with astonished acclaim.

In this revised and expanded edition of his now classic debut, Prokofieff investigates the deepest mysteries of Rudolf Steiner's life and individuality and his establishing of the new mysteries on earth in the twentieth century. He examines the earthly and supersensible aspects of the first Goetheanum, the implications of the Christmas Conference of 1923–24, and the Foundation Stone meditation which Rudolf Steiner left as a legacy to the Anthroposophical Society.

480 pp; 24 × 16 cm; hardback; ISBN 0 904693 61 9

RUDOLF STEINER'S RESEARCH INTO KARMA AND THE MISSION OF THE ANTHROPOSOPHICAL SOCIETY

Sergei O. Prokofieff

In this inspiring lecture addressed to the anthroposophical movement Prokofieff explains why true modern Christian research into karma does not arise out of intellectual speculation, curiosity, or nebulous mystical experiences. The process of karmic research based on spiritual science should lead to a fundamental transformation of our human nature, enabling a full experience of the cosmos within which we exist.

Giving an overview of how the spiritual hierarchies and Christ, the Lord of Karma, work in the ordering of human karma, Prokofieff leads us to the karma and mission of the Anthroposophical Society, indicating what must come about—before the end of the century—if this karmic mission is to be fulfilled.

48 pp; 21.5 × 13.5 cm; paperback; ISBN 0 904693 69 4

ABOUT THE AUTHOR

Sergei O. Prokofieff was born in Moscow in 1954, where he studied Fine Arts and Painting at the Moscow School of Art. At an early age he came across the work of the Austrian-born philosopher and seer Rudolf Steiner, and soon realised that his life was to be dedicated to the Christian path of esoteric knowledge. He currently works as a writer and international lecturer, and is involved in developing anthroposophical work in Russia.